Pick of the Seasons

Quilts to Inspire You Through the Year

BY TAMMY JOHNSON AND AVIS SHIRER
OF JOINED AT THE HIP

KANSAS CITY STAR
QUILTS
Continuing the Tradition

Pick of the Seasons
Quilts to Inspire You Through the Year

BY TAMMY JOHNSON AND AVIS SHIRER
OF JOINED AT THE HIP

Edited by Judy Pearlstein
Tech Edited Christina DeArmond
Book Design by Amy Robertson
Quilt Photographs by Aaron Leimkuehler
Illustrations by Eric Sears
Production Assistance by Jo Ann Groves

Published by Kansas City Star Books
1729 Grand Boulevard
Kansas City, Missouri 64108

First edition, first printing
ISBN: 978-1-935362-16-6
Library of Congress number: 2009929545

Printed in the United States of America
By Walsworth Publishing Co.
Marceline, Missouri

To order copies, call StarInfo, (816) 234-4636.
(Say "Operator.")

The Quilter's Home Page

Contents

About the Authors

Avis Shirer and Tammy Johnson have self-published 12 quilt books and over 250 patterns in the 13 years they have been in business. They have also designed six lines of fabric for Clothworks. In their whimsical designs, they love to combine piecing with appliqué and then add touches of wool, rickrack and buttons to complete the look. For more information about their books and patterns, visit **joinedatthehip.com**.

Acknowledgments

- We would like to thank Sue Urich for her wonderful machine quilting. Sue's work adds the final, magic touch that brings our quilts to life.
- We would like to thank Doug Weaver of Kansas City Star Books for the opportunity to work with him and his staff.
- We would like to thank our editor, Judy Pearlstein, book designer, Amy Robertson, and photographer, Aaron Leimkuehler, for their expertise in helping us though the process and for their great vision in putting together a beautiful book.

Introduction

We have four distinct seasons in North Iowa. It makes life here interesting. Spring can be cold, windy and rainy, and sometimes even has a few flakes of snow. We get very excited when we see the trees starting to bud and the tulips pushing through the ground — signs that there is life after a long, cold winter. Summer brings forth hot, humid temperatures and lots of bright, sunny skies. The days are long and hours are spent on the porch sipping tall glasses of lemonade. Fall is the time of the year when the earth bursts with ripe fruits from the summer growing season and cooling temperatures. The leaves on the trees give us a colorful show in shades of yellow, orange and red. Winter ushers in bitter, cold winds and snow. As the years pass, we aren't nearly as excited about a good old Iowa snow storm as we were when we were kids, but it is quite a beautiful sight after we have received a fresh blanket of snow. It looks like a blanket of diamonds under the light of the sun and the moon. Spring comes and the cycle starts again. In this book, we've combined our favorite motifs and colors of each of the seasons to bring you the cream of the crop. Stitch up these projects to decorate your home throughout the year — these projects are the pick of the season!

— *Avis and Tammy*

General Directions

Seam Allowances

Please use a ¼" seam allowance for all of the projects. The seam allowance is included in the measurements given for rotary cutting. There is no seam allowance included on the appliqué templates. If you prefer to use hand appliqué, you will need to add the seam allowance to the appliqué shapes.

Stitch and Flip

We use the Stitch and Flip technique in many of the projects in this book. This is a simple technique that gives the look of working with triangles when only squares and rectangles are used.

Cut the pieces to the appropriate sizes. Lay the square on top of the base square or rectangle. Stitch diagonally across the square in the direction indicated.

We prefer to trim the corner of the upper square only. This way, if your diagonal stitching wasn't accurate, you will still have the base piece intact to use for an accurate seam allowance.

Turn the resulting triangle over the seam and press.

Fusible Appliqué

We like to use fusible appliqué to make these projects fast and easy. Please refer to the manufacturer's directions on your favorite fusible product for more information. The templates in this book have been reversed for fusible appliqué. Trace the number of shapes as indicated on each template onto the smooth, paper side of the fusible web. Remember to leave about ½" between traced shapes. Cut around the shapes, approximately ¼" outside of the traced line. Fuse the shape to the wrong side of the appropriate fabric. Cut the shape out on the traced line. Position onto the foundation piece and iron in place. We prefer to position most of the appliqué shapes before we iron in place so that we can adjust the placement if necessary. We then stitch around all of the appliqué shapes with a machine blanket stitch using thread that matches the appliqué shape. If your machine doesn't have a blanket stitch, a zigzag stitch would also work.

Binding

We like to use single-fold binding to finish the quilt edges. Cut 1 ½" wide strips across the width of the binding fabric to make single-fold binding. Join the strips to make one strip long enough to go all the way around the quilt plus at least 10" for turning the corners and finishing the ends. If you prefer a wider binding, please adjust the fabric requirements as needed.

Begin in the middle of the bottom edge of the quilt. Lay the binding strip on the quilt top with right sides together and raw edges even. Start stitching 1" from the end of the binding strip. Stop stitching ¼" from the corner of the quilt. Turn the quilt so you can sew down the next side. Fold the binding strip up, forming a 45 degree angle. Bring the binding down on itself and stitch down this side of the quilt. Repeat at all four corners.

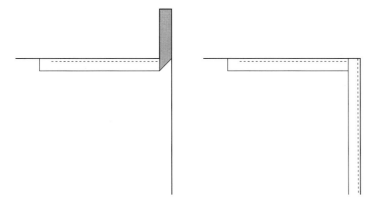

When you are close to the beginning of the binding, fold back the 1" tail that was left at the start of the binding and continue to stitch through all three layers. Turn the binding to the back of the quilt. Turn under ¼" on the raw edge and slipstitch in place by hand.

Spring

❁

Springtime on the Square

58" x 92"

The Log Cabin block is one of my favorites. There are so many variations in the construction and color placement. In this quilt, we alternated wide logs and narrow logs. To add more interest, the placement of the colors was alternated in every other block. The pinks, reds and browns remind me of my flowering crabapple tree when it is in full bloom in the spring – it just makes me smile.

FABRIC REQUIREMENTS

1/3 yard each of at least eight different brown prints

1/3 yard each of at least eight different red-pink prints

1 yard of a light print for the sashing strips and inner border

1 1/2 yards of brown print for the outer border and binding

INSTRUCTIONS

Pink Blocks

(These are the blocks with the wide pink logs.)

- Make 8 blocks. Finished size – 16"

For each pink block:

- Cut 1 – 2½" square from pink #1 – piece A
- Cut 2 – 1½" x 2½" from brown #1 – piece B
- Cut 2 – 1½" x 4½" from brown #1 – piece C
- Cut 2 – 2½" x 4½" from pink #2 – piece D
- Cut 2 – 2½" x 8½" from pink #2 – piece E
- Cut 2 – 1½" x 8½" from brown #2 – piece F
- Cut 2 – 1½" x 10½" from brown #2 – piece G
- Cut 2 – 2½" x 10½" from pink #3 – piece H
- Cut 2 – 2½" x 14½" from pink #3 – piece I
- Cut 2 – 1½" x 14½" from brown #3 – piece |
- Cut 2 – 1½" x 16½" from brown #3 – piece K
- Begin by sewing a brown B piece to each side of the pink A square. Add the brown C pieces to the top and bottom. Sew the pink D pieces to the sides and then add the pink E piece to the top and bottom. Continue in this matter as shown in the block diagram.

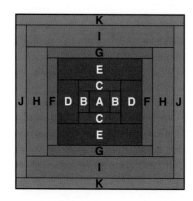

Springtime on the Square
Made by Tammy Johnson; Quilted by Sue Urich, Garner, Iowa
58" x 92"

Springtime on the Square continued

Brown Blocks

(These are the blocks with the wide brown logs.)

❋ Make 7 blocks. Finished size – 16"

For each brown block:

❋ Cut 1 – 2½" square from brown #1 – piece A

❋ Cut 2 – 1½" x 2½" from pink #1 – piece B

❋ Cut 2 – 1½" x 4½" from pink #1 – piece C

❋ Cut 2 – 2½" x 4½" from brown #2 – piece D

❋ Cut 2 – 2½" x 8½" from brown #2 – piece E

❋ Cut 2 – 1½" x 8½" from pink #2 – piece F

❋ Cut 2 – 1½" x 10½" from pink #2 – piece G

❋ Cut 2 – 2½" x 10½" from brown #3 – piece H

❋ Cut 2 – 2½" x 14½" from brown #3 – piece I

❋ Cut 2 – 1½" x 14½" from pink #3 – piece J

❋ Cut 2 – 1½" x 16½" from pink #3 – piece K

❋ Construct these blocks in the same manner as the pink blocks, referring to the block diagram.

Assembly

❋ Cut 10 – 1½" x 16½" rectangles from the light print for the vertical sashing strips. Cut five 1½" strips across the width of the light print. From these strips, piece together four 1½" x 50½" rectangles for the horizontal sashing strips. Sew the blocks and the sashing strips together in five rows having three blocks and two vertical sashing strips in each row. Sew the rows and the four horizontal sashing strips together alternately. Refer to the quilt diagram on page 13.

Borders

❋ Cut seven 1½" strips across the width of the light print fabric. From these strips, piece together two 1½" x 50½" rectangles and sew to the top and bottom of the quilt. Piece together two 1½" x 86½" rectangles and sew to the sides of the quilt. For the outer border, cut eight 3½" strips across the width of the brown border fabric. Piece together two 3½" x 52½" rectangles and sew to the top and bottom of the quilt. Piece together two 3½" x 92½" rectangles and sew to the sides of the quilt. Quilt as desired and bind. Refer to page 7 for binding instructions.

Edna's Vines

48" x 60"

Edna was a dear lady who lived down the street from us. She had the most beautiful clematis vine growing on the front of her house. What a beautiful sight it was when it was in bloom! How I wish I could grow one just like it.

FABRIC REQUIREMENTS

1/4 yard each of 10 assorted coral fabrics
   for star blocks, flower appliqués
   and border strips
1 1/4 yards of tan print for star block background
1 1/3 yards of pink check
1/4 yard of pink and tan stripe
1/4 yard of green print for flower appliqués
1/2 yard of coral stripe for binding
3 1/4 yards of 1 3/4" wide green rickrack
2 yards of 1/2" wide ecru rickrack
1 yard of fusible web

INSTRUCTIONS

Block Construction

❋ Make 9 blocks. Finished size – 8" x 16"

For each block:

❋ Cut one 5 1/4" square, bisected twice to yield 4 triangles, from tan print
❋ Cut one 4 1/2" square from tan print
❋ Cut two 2 1/2" x 4 1/2" from tan print
❋ Cut four 2 1/2" x 6 1/2" from tan print
❋ Cut four 2 1/2" squares from tan print
❋ Cut one 5 1/4" square, bisected twice to yield 4 triangles, from coral
❋ Cut two 2 1/2" x 4 1/2" from coral
❋ Cut four 2 1/2" squares from pink check
❋ Stitch together a tan triangle and a coral triangle. Repeat to make two and then sew the two units together as shown. Make two units like this.

❋ Sew these two triangle units to the top and bottom of the 4 1/2" tan square. Then add a tan 2 1/2" x 4 1/2" piece to the top and bottom as shown.

Edna's Vines
Made by Tammy Johnson; Quilted by Sue Urich
48" x 60"

✳ Make a Flying Geese unit by laying a tan 2½" square on top of a coral 2½" x 4½" piece. Stitch and flip, following the directions on page 6. Repeat with another tan 2½" square as shown. Repeat to make two of these Flying Geese units.

✳ Lay a pink 2½" square on top of a tan 2½" x 6½" rectangle. Stitch and flip. Repeat to make two. Lay a pink 2½" square on the opposite end of a tan 2½" x 6½" piece. Stitch and flip again, making two units like this.

Make 2 like this.   Make 2 like this.

✳ Sew two of the above units to each end of a Flying Geese unit. Repeat to make two as shown. Then add to the sides of the previously sewn unit to complete the block.

Assemble the Vertical Block Strips

✳ Cut six 2 ½" x 8 ½" rectangles and six 1 ½" x 8 ½" rectangles from the pink check. Sew together three star blocks and two pink 2 ½" x 8 ½" pieces alternately. Add a pink 1 ½" x 8 ½" rectangle to the top and bottom of this vertical block strip. Repeat to make three strips like this.

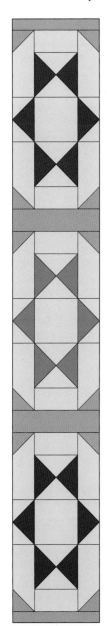

Edna's Vines continued

Cut six 3½" wide strips across the width of the pink check fabric. Piece these strips together to make four 54½" long strips. Cut three 2½" wide strips across the width of the pink striped fabric. Piece these strips together to make two 54½" long strips. Sew two 3½" wide strips and one 2½" wide strip together alternately. Make two of these units. Lay the 1¾" wide green rickrack down the center of the strips and sew close to the edges of the rickrack using a straight stitch by machine and matching thread.

Sew the vertical block strips and the rickrack strips together alternately. Cut three 1½" wide strips across the width of the pink check. Piece together to make two 54½" long strips. Sew these strips to the sides of the quilt.

Applique the Flowers

(Templates on page 62)

❋ Refer to the fusible appliqué directions on page 6. Prepare 10 flower appliqués. Position the green flower base so that the end is tucked in a curve of the rickrack. Position the flower head, tucking the bottom edge under the flower base. Do not fuse in place yet. Position the ½" wide ecru rickrack so that the bottom edge of the rickrack is under the green flower base. Turn the raw ends of the rickrack under the flower. When you are happy with the placement, fuse in place. It may help to flip the rickrack over at a 90 degree angle at the middle "crook" for ease of placement.

Add the Border

Cut the following rectangles from assorted coral fabrics and stitch to the quilt as follows:

❋ Cut one 3 ½" x 26 ½" rectangle and one 3 ½" x 16 ½" rectangle.
❋ Sew together and stitch to the top of the quilt.
❋ Cut one 3 ½" x 26 ½" rectangle and one 3 ½" x 31 ½" rectangle.
❋ Sew together and stitch to the right hand side of the quilt.
❋ Cut one 3 ½" x 26 ½" rectangle and one 3 ½" x 19 ½" rectangle.
❋ Sew together and stitch to the bottom of the quilt.
❋ Cut one 3 ½" x 25 ½" rectangle and one 3 ½" x 35 ½" rectangle.
❋ Sew together and stitch to the left side of the quilt.
❋ Quilt as desired and bind, referring to the binding directions on page 7.

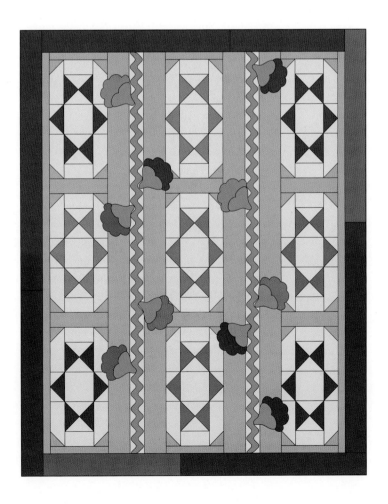

Spring Blooms

Frame size – 11 ¾" x 36"

There's nothing better than seeing the first blooms of spring after a long, cold Iowa winter. We used soft yellows and creams and a touch of rickrack to depict that spring scene in this framed piece. It will surely bring a breath of spring into your home.

SUPPLIES

1/2 yard of golden brown
    coarsely woven fabric such as silk matka
6" x 12" piece of tan checked wool or cotton
    for vase
7" squares of two yellow wools or cottons
    for flowers and accents on the center flower
7" x 10" piece of cream wool or cotton
    for center flower, flower accents
    and small circle flowers
2" x 11" piece of dark green wool or cotton
    for long stems
4" x 7" piece of light green wool or cotton
    for short stems
4" square of green checked wool or cotton
    for leaves
3 1/8 yards of 1/2" wide ecru rickrack
Gold embroidery floss
1 yard of fusible web
11 3/4" x 36" piece of batting
Chalk marking pencil
Poster frame with an 11 3/4" x 36" opening

INSTRUCTIONS

Prepare the Foundation

Cut a 11 ¾" x 36" rectangle from the golden brown fabric. Measure in 1 ¾" from the edges of the rectangle and mark with a chalk pencil. Lay the rickrack on the long vertical lines first and pin in place. Stitch down the center of the rickrack using a straight stitch by machine and matching thread. Lay the rickrack on the short horizontal lines and stitch in place as before.

Appliqué

(Templates on pages 63, 64)

We used fusible appliqué throughout this project. Refer to the fusible appliqué directions on page 6. Do not fuse anything in place until you have positioned all of the appliqués. Position the vase, centering it approximately 3" up from the bottom row of rickrack. Prepare the long stem pieces by drawing a 2" x 11" rectangle on the paper side of the fusible web. Cut the rectangle out on the drawn line and fuse to the dark green wool. With a rotary cutter, cut one ⅜" x 5 ½" strip for the stem on the left, cut one ⅜" x 10" strip for the center stem, and cut one ⅜" x 7 ½" strip for the stem on the right. Position the stems, tucking the bottom ends under the vase. Refer to the color photo for placement help. Next, add the leaf units and the large flower heads. Add the flower accents. Position the two short stems, curving them gently as shown. Finally, add seven circle flowers to each of the two short stems. The template page will help you with placement. When you are happy with the placement, fuse in place. Using three strands of gold embroidery floss, stitch in the center of each of the circle flowers as shown. Stitch around the rest of the appliqués using a machine blanket stitch and matching thread.

Lay the frame face down on the floor. Insert the appliquéd piece face down and then lay the batting on top of the appliquéd piece. Put the frame back in place. Hang and enjoy!

Spring Blooms Framed Art
Made by Tammy Johnson
Frame size – 11 ¾" x 36"

Summer

Dahlia

36" square

There is nothing prettier in a summer garden than an assortment of dahlias. The color is very intense and they seem to thrive in the hot sun.

FABRIC REQUIREMENTS

1 1/8 yards of background fabric for basket foundation, rickrack foundation and flowers

1/4 yard each of 4 assorted yellows for Four Patch blocks

1/4 yard each of 4 assorted reds for Four Patch blocks, flower appliqués and binding (Binding and appliqués will take 1/4 yard.)

Scrap of yellow for the flower centers

1/3 yard of brown for basket

1/4 yard of green for stems and leaves

1 yard of fusible web

4 3/4 yards of 1 3/4" wide red rickrack

Batting and backing measuring 42" square

INSTRUCTIONS

Appliquéd Blocks

(Templates on page 65, 66)

✸ Construct the center basket block first. Cut a 12½" square from the background fabric. We used fusible appliqué throughout this project. Refer to page 6 for more information on fusible appliqué. Position all of the appliqué shapes before fusing them in place. Begin by centering the basket shape ¼" up from the bottom, raw edge of the background square. Next, add the stems, leaves and flowers, tucking the ends of the stems under the basket. Some of the leaves and flowers overlap the basket. Refer to the color photo for placement help. When you are happy with the placement, fuse in place.

✸ For the four flower blocks, cut four 4½" squares from the background fabric. Prepare the appliqué shapes, noting that you will need to reverse the templates for two of the blocks. Position the stem first, placing it approximately ¼" up from the raw edge. Add the flower, covering the upper end of the stem. Add the flower center and leaves. When you are happy with the placement, fuse in place.

Rickrack Strips

To make the eight rickrack strips, cut the following pieces from the background fabric:

✸ Cut 2 – 2½" x 12½" – piece A

✸ Cut 2 – 2½" x 16½" – piece B

✸ Cut 2 – 2½" x 24½" – piece C

✸ Cut 2 – 2½" x 28½" – piece D

✸ Cut the red rickrack the same length as the fabric strips. Center the rickrack on the strip and stitch close to both edges with a straight stitch by machine and matching thread. Stitch an A strip to the top and bottom of the appliquéd basket block. Then stitch a B strip to the sides. Set the C and D strips aside.

Dahlia
Made by Avis Shirer
36" square

Four Patch Blocks

- Make 48 blocks. Finished size – 4" square.

Cut the following:

- 96 – 2 ½" squares from assorted red fabrics – piece A
- 96 – 2 ½" squares from assorted yellow fabrics – piece B
- Stitch 2 A squares and 2 B squares together as shown. Repeat to make 48 blocks.

- Stitch together 4 Four Patch blocks. Repeat to make four of these units. Stitch two of the units to the top and bottom of the quilt. Sew an appliquéd flower block to each end of the remaining Four Patch units. Sew these units to the sides of the quilt.
- Next, add a rickrack C strip to the top and bottom of the quilt. Sew a rickrack D strip to the sides.
- Sew together 7 Four Patch blocks. Repeat to make 2 units. Sew to the top and bottom of the quilt. Sew together 9 Four Patch blocks. Repeat to make 2 units. Sew these units to the sides of the quilt. Quilt as desired and bind referring to page 7 for binding instructions.

Sheep in the Meadow

41" x 56"

When I was growing up on the farm, we didn't have sheep in the meadow – we had cows. But I can imagine summer days, herding the sheep from one place to another. Of course, my trusty dog, Curly, would have been by my side, helping with the task.

FABRIC REQUIREMENTS

1 yard of tan print for sheep block background

1/2 yard of tan check for tree blocks

1/2 yard of cream solid for sheep

1/4 yard of black solid for sheep's legs, heads, ears and tails

1/8 yard of black mini check for circle appliqués

1/8 yard of gold print for star appliqués

1/8 yard cuts of 5 assorted red prints for checkerboard blocks

1/4 yard cuts of 4 assorted green prints for tree blocks

1/3 yard of brown for tree blocks

1 yard of black and gold print for sashing strips and border

1/2 yard of black for binding

1 yard of fusible web

Batting and backing measuring 47"x 62"

INSTRUCTIONS

Sheep Blocks

✿ Make 5 blocks. Finished size – 13" x 15"

Construct the lower portion of the block first. For each block:

✿ Cut 1 – 6 ½" x 10 ½" from the cream solid – piece A

✿ Cut 1 – 2 ½" x 13 ½" from the tan print – piece B

✿ Cut 1 – 2 ½" x 4 ½" from the tan print – piece C

✿ Cut 1 – 2 ½" square from the tan print – piece D

✿ Cut 5 – 1 ½" x 2 ½" from the tan print – piece E

✿ Cut 1 – 1 ½" x 8 ½" from the tan print – piece F

✿ Cut 1 – 1 ½" x 3 ½" from the tan print – piece G

✿ Cut 6 – 1 ½" squares from the tan print – piece H

✿ Cut 1 – 1 ½" x 3 ½" from the black solid – piece I

✿ Cut 4 – 1 ½" x 2 ½" from the black solid – piece J

✿ Begin by placing a tan H square on the corner of the cream A piece. Stitch and flip, following the directions on page 6. Repeat on all 4 corners of the cream A piece as shown.

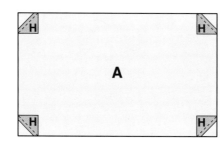 

Sheep in the Meadow
Made by Tammy Johnson; Quilted by Sue Urich; 41" x 56"

✽ Stitch together four tan E pieces, one tan D piece and four black J pieces as shown. Sew this unit to the bottom of the previously sewn unit.

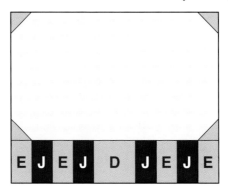

✽ Add the tan F piece to the left side of 3 of the blocks and to the right side of 2 of the blocks.

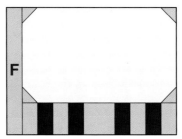 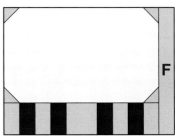

Make 3 like this. Make 2 like this.

✽ Lay a tan H square on the black I piece. Stitch and flip as shown. Repeat with another tan H square on the other corner. Add a tan G piece as shown.

✽ Add a tan E piece to the top and a tan C piece to the bottom of this unit. Reverse the middle section as shown on two of the blocks.

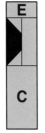 

Make 3 like this. Make 2 like this.

⚙ Stitch this unit to the appropriate body unit. Then add a tan B piece to the top to complete the lower portion of the blocks.

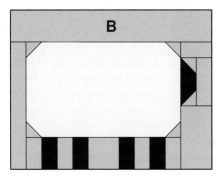

Make 3 like this.

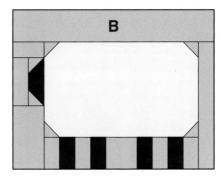

Make 2 like this.

Now construct the upper checkerboard portion of the blocks. For each block:

⚙ Cut 2 – 1½" x 12" rectangles from a red print – piece A

⚙ Cut 1 – 1½" x 6" rectangle from a red print – piece B

⚙ Cut 8 – 1½" square from a red print – piece C

⚙ Cut 1 – 1½" x 12" rectangle from the tan print – piece D

⚙ Cut 2 – 1½" x 6" rectangle from the tan print – piece E

⚙ Cut 10 – 1½" x 3½" rectangles from the tan print – piece F

⚙ Sew together the two A pieces and one D piece. Sew together two E pieces and one B piece. Press the seams towards the red fabric on both strips. Cut these strip units into 1½" slices. Cut six slices from the A-D unit and three slices from the B-E unit.

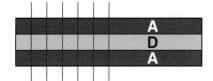   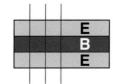

⚙ Sew these slices together as shown and add a tan F piece to the top and bottom. Make three units like this.

⚙ Sew a red C square to both ends of a tan F piece. Make 4 of these units. Sew these units and the previously sewn units together as shown. Then add this checkerboard unit to the top of the sheep unit.

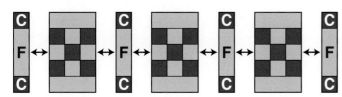

Appliqué

(Templates on page 67)

⚙ We used fusible appliqué for this project. Follow the directions on page 6 for help with fusible appliqué. Appliqué the ear and tail, noting that you will use the same template for both shapes. Next, appliqué the black mini-check circle and then the gold star.

Tree Blocks

⚙ Make 4 blocks. Finished size – 9" x 15"

For each block:

⚙ Cut 1 – 8½" x 9½" rectangle from the tan check – piece A

⚙ Cut 4 – 2½" squares from the tan check – piece B

⚙ Cut 1 – 7½" x 9½" rectangle from green print – piece C

⚙ Lay a B square on top of the C piece. Stitch and flip, referring to the instructions on page 6. Repeat on all 4 corners. Add the tan A piece to the bottom.

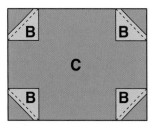
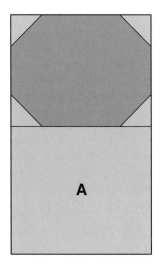

⚙ Appliqué the tree trunk to the block. Note that you will add 4" to the bottom of the template when tracing. Position the tree trunk so that it is centered on the block and the bottom raw edges are even. Fuse in place.

Assemble the Blocks

- Stitch together a right-facing sheep block, a tree block and a left-facing sheep block. Make 2 rows like this. (See photo.)

- Cut two 2½" x 15½" rectangles from the black and gold print. Cut two 3" x 35½" strips from the black and gold print.

- Stitch together 2 tree blocks, a right-facing sheep block and the two 2½" x 15½" strips as shown. Then add the 3" x 35½" strips to the top and bottom.

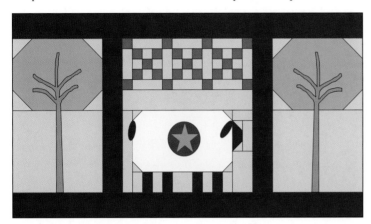

- Sew the two previously sewn rows to the top and bottom of this unit.

Borders

- Cut 2 – 3½" x 35½" strips from the black and gold print. Sew to the top and bottom of the quilt. Cut three 3½" wide strips across the width of the black and gold print. Sew the strips together and cut two 3½" x 56½" rectangles. Sew to the sides of the quilt. Quilt as desired and bind. For binding help, refer to page 7.

Liberty Garden

Frame Size – 11 ¾" x 36"

I love the 4th of July! It is a fun summer holiday (and I celebrate my birthday, as well. Pretty cool indeed to have fireworks and parades!) I am often struck by the beauty of the coneflowers. The color is so vibrant and this flower almost bakes in the hot July sun. This framed art is a tribute to summer's best — 4th of July celebrations and the coneflower.

FABRIC REQUIREMENTS

1/4 yard of light background fabric for the center section

1/4 yard of navy blue for the star field

1/8 yard of gold for the star appliqués

1/8 yard of green for stem and leaf appliqués

1/8 yard of brown for flower centers

1/8 yard each of 3 assorted purples for flowers

1/3 yard of teal blue plaid for watering can

1/8 yard of black for letter appliqués

1/3 yard of red for flag border

1/4 yard of medium background fabric for flag border

1/8 yard brown plaid for trim on watering can

1 yard of fusible web

11 3/4" x 36" piece of batting

Poster frame with an 11 3/4" x 36" opening

INSTRUCTIONS

Cutting Instructions

✺ Cut 1 – 6 ½" x 30 ½" from the light background fabric – piece A.

✺ Cut 1 – 3 ½" x 12 ½" from the navy blue fabric – piece B.

✺ Cut 1 – 3 ½" x 6 ½" from the navy blue fabric – piece C.

✺ Cut 1 – 3 ½" x 12 ½" from the red fabric – piece D.

✺ Cut 9 – 3 ½" squares from the red fabric – piece E.

✺ Cut 9 – 3 ½" squares from the medium background fabric – piece F.

✺ For the left side border, sew together a row of four E squares and four F squares alternately. Add the C piece to this strip. For the right side border, sew together a row of five E squares and five F squares alternately. Add these strips to sides of the light A piece. Then add the B piece to the top and the D piece to the bottom.

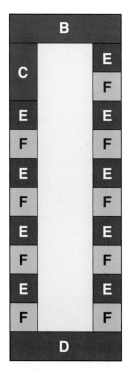

Liberty Garden Framed Art
Made by Avis Shirer
Frame Size – 11 ³/₄" x 36"

Appliqué

(Templates on page 68–70)

- We used fusible appliqué throughout this project. Refer to page 6 for help with fusible appliqué. Begin by positioning the main portion of the watering can. There is no template for this piece. Draw a 4 ½" x 13 ¼" rectangle on the paper side of the fusible web. Cut outside of the drawn line and fuse to the wrong side of the teal blue plaid. Cut on the drawn line and position onto the foundation, referring to the color photo for placement help. Next, add the handle and spout, tucking the edges under the main portion of the watering can. Add the leaves, flowers and stars. When you are happy with the placement, fuse in place. Add four watering can accents, which are ¾" x 4 ½" rectangles. Again, there are no templates for these. Repeat the process for the main portion of the watering can for these pieces. Fuse in place. Next, add the word "Liberty" and the large border stars. Position these stars close to the inner edge of the border to keep the stars from being cut off when framed.
- Lay the frame face down on the floor. Insert the appliquéd piece face down and then lay the batting on top of the appliquéd piece. Put the frame back in place. Hang and enjoy!

Fall

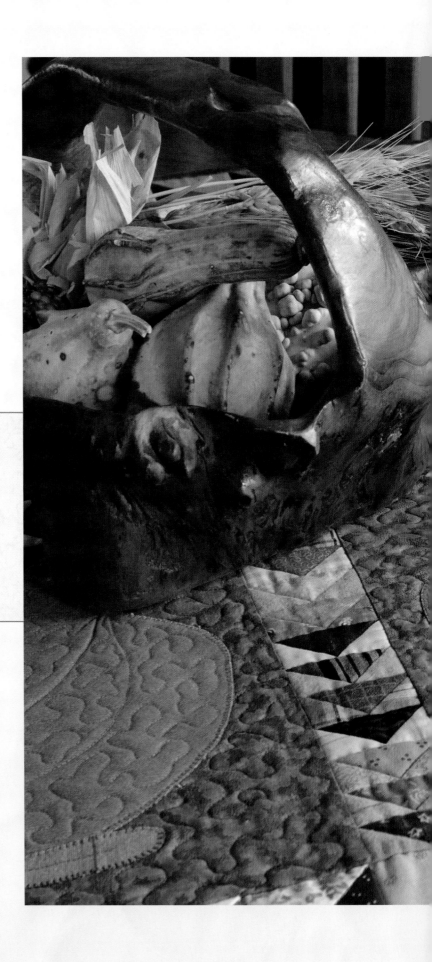

Pumpkins and Acorns Galore

34" square

Fall is my favorite time of the year! I love to celebrate the season by visiting Pikes Peak along the Mississippi River. The sky is such a brilliant blue and the leaves on the trees are every shade of orange, red and gold. There is a path that leads to the lookout area where visitors can gaze down at the Mississippi River. The trail that leads to this path is covered with thousands of acorns that have fallen from the mighty oak trees. It is also a great area to catch a glimpse of a bald eagle. This table square celebrates the fall season!

FABRIC REQUIREMENTS

7/8 yard of teal blue for pumpkin blocks

1/3 yard of orange for pumpkin appliqués

1/8 yard of green for pumpkin leaf appliqués

1/8 yard of brown for pumpkin stem appliqués

Scraps of assorted background fabrics
for Flying Geese blocks and acorn blocks
to equal 7/8 yard

Scraps of assorted medium to dark fabrics
for Flying Geese blocks to equal 7/8 yard

1/3 yard of brown print for binding

1/8 yard of two brown fabrics for acorns
and caps

1 1/2 yards of fusible web

Batting and backing measuring 38" square

INSTRUCTIONS

Pumpkin Blocks

(Templates on pages 71, 72)

- Make 4 blocks. Finished size – 12" square.
- Cut four 12½" squares from the teal blue fabric. Appliqué a pumpkin to each of these squares. We used fusible appliqué throughout this project. For help with fusible appliqué, refer to page 6. Refer to the color photo for placement help. Note that the pumpkin is placed on the diagonal on the block. Position the pumpkin first. Add the stem and then the leaf. When you are happy with the placement, fuse in place.

Acorn Blocks

- Make 4 blocks. Finished size – 4"
- Cut four 4½" squares from a background fabric. Position the bottom portion of the acorn on the square and then add the acorn cap. Note that the acorn is placed on the diagonal on this block also. Make sure that the acorn shape is at least ¼" away from the edges of the block to allow for the seam allowances. When you are happy with the placement, fuse in place.

Flying Geese Blocks

- Make 48 blocks. Finished size – 1" x 2"
- Cut 96 – 1½" squares from assorted background fabrics, piece A.
- Cut 48 – 1½" x 2½" rectangles from assorted medium to dark fabrics, piece B.
- Lay an A square on top of a B piece. Stitch and flip following the directions on page 6. Repeat with another A square. Repeat to make 48 blocks.

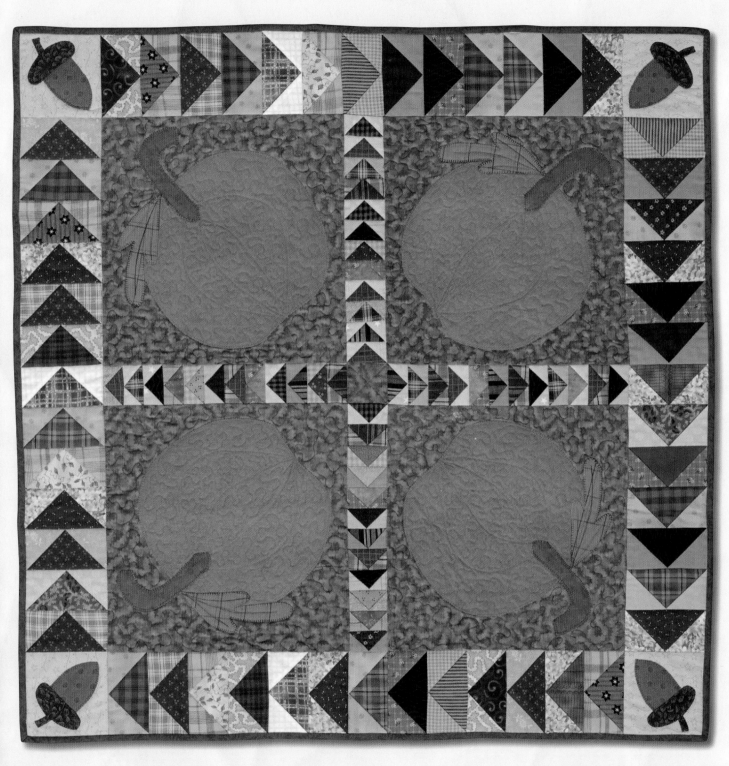

Pumpkins and Acorns Galore
Made by Avis Shirer
34" square

Pumpkins and Acorns Galore continued

🍂 Stitch these Flying Geese blocks together in four sets of 12 blocks each. Sew one of these units between two of the pumpkin blocks. Repeat to make two like this. Cut a 2½" square from the teal blue fabric. Stitch a Flying Geese unit to each side of this square. Sew these units together as shown.

Outer Border Flying Geese Blocks

🍂 Make 52 blocks. Finished size – 2" x 4"

🍂 Cut 104 – 2½" squares from assorted background fabrics.

🍂 Cut 52 – 2½" x 4½" rectangles from assorted medium to dark fabrics.

🍂 In the same manner as before, construct 52 Flying Geese blocks.

🍂 Stitch these blocks together in four sets of 13 blocks each. Sew two of these strips to the top and bottom of the quilt. Sew an acorn block to each end of the two remaining Flying Geese strips. Sew these units to the sides of the quilt. Quilt as desired and bind. For binding help, please refer to page 7 .

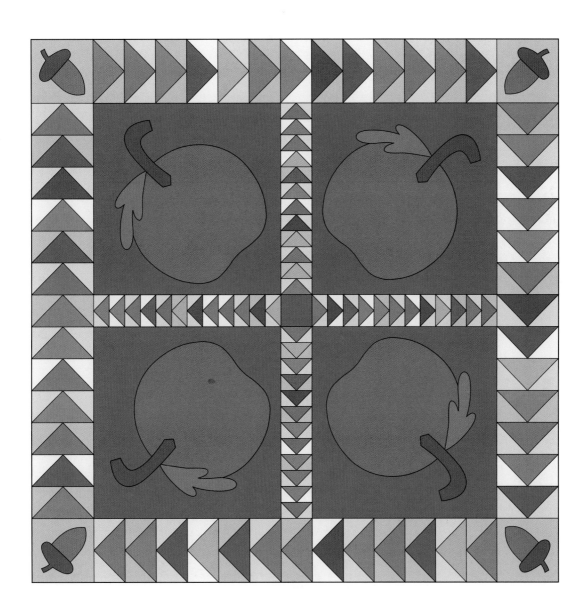

Harvest Moon

48" x 56"

Easy appliqué and basic blocks make this quilt a snap. The orange and teal fabrics are very striking in this quilt.

FABRIC REQUIREMENTS

2/3 yard of tan fabric for Square-in-a-Square blocks

1/2 yard of light blue and gold print
   for Square-in-a-Square blocks and inner border

2/3 yard of brown print for Four Patch blocks

2/3 yard of rust print for Four Patch blocks
   and small circle appliqués

1/2 yard of gold print for large circle appliqués

1 1/2 yards of blue print for Square-in-a-Square blocks,
   small circle appliqués, outer border and binding

Batting and backing measuring 54" x 62"

INSTRUCTIONS

Four Patch Blocks

🍁 Make 15 blocks. Finished size – 8" square.

🍁 Cut 30 – 4½" squares from the rust fabric – piece A.

🍁 Cut 30 – 4½" squares from the brown print – piece B.

🍁 Stitch two A squares and two B squares together as shown. Repeat to make 15 blocks.

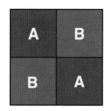

Square in a Square Blocks

🍁 Make 15 blocks. Finished size – 8" square.

🍁 Cut 15 – 4½" squares from the light blue and gold print – piece A.

🍁 Cut 15 – 5¼" squares, bisected twice to yield 60 triangles, from the blue print – piece B.

🍁 Cut 30 – 4⅞" squares, bisected once to yield 60 triangles, from the tan fabric – piece C.

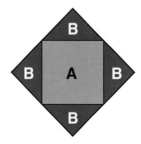

Harvest Moon
Made by Avis Shirer
48" x 56"

Harvest Moon continued

- Sew four B triangles to the A square.
- Add four C triangles to the block as shown.

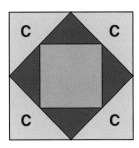

Appliqué

(Templates on page 73)

- We used fusible appliqué throughout this project. Refer to page 6 for more information on fusible appliqué. Trace 45 of the A circle shapes and fuse to the gold fabric. Trace 45 B circle shapes and fuse 30 to the blue fabric and 15 to the rust fabric.
- Appliqué a gold A circle to each of the rust squares in the Four-Patch blocks. Add a blue B circle, centering it on top of the gold circle.
- Appliqué a gold A circle on the center of the Square-in-a-Square blocks. Add a rust B circle on top, centering it on top of the gold circle.

Borders

- Sew the blocks together in 6 rows of 5 blocks each following the quilt diagram. Cut 2 – 1½" x 40½" strips from the light blue and gold print. Sew to the top and bottom of the quilt. Cut 3 – 1½" strips across the width of the light blue and gold print. Piece together and cut 2 – 1½" x 50½" strips and sew to the sides of the quilt.
- For the outer border, cut 2 – 3½" x 42½" strips from the blue print. Sew to the top and bottom of the quilt. Cut 3 – 3½" strips across the width of the blue print fabric. Piece together and cut 2 – 3½" x 56½" strips and sew to the sides. Quilt as desired and bind. For more help on binding, refer to page 7.

Harvest Framed Art

Frame Size – 11 ¾" x 36"

*Isn't fall a wonderful time of the year? It is filled with bright, vibrant colors.
It is also the time for harvesting all of the earth's bounty. This wonderful framed art celebrates
this special time of the year.*

FABRIC REQUIREMENTS

1/3 yard of taupe fabric for the background

1/3 yard of medium blue for the outer border

1/8 yard of black for letter appliqués

1/4 yard of gold for the sunflower appliqués

1/8 yard of black print for the sunflower centers

1/8 yard of green for flower stem and leaf appliqués

1/8 yard different green for cattail stems

1/3 yard of orange for pumpkin appliqué

1/8 yard of orange for pumpkin accent

1/8 yard of brown for cattail appliqués

1 yard of fusible web

11 3/4" x 36" piece of batting

Poster frame with an 11 3/4" x 36" opening

INSTRUCTIONS

🍂 Cut 1 – 8 ½" x 32 ½" rectangle from the taupe fabric. Cut 2 – 2 ½" x 8 ½" rectangles from the blue fabric and sew to the top and bottom of the taupe rectangle.

🍂 Cut 2 – 2 ½" x 36 ½" from the blue fabric and sew to the sides.

Appliqué

(Templates on pages 74–76)

🍂 We used fusible appliqué throughout this project. Refer to page 6 for more help with fusible appliqué. Position the pumpkin first. Add the pumpkin accent at the top, tucking the lower edge under the pumpkin. Next, position the stems, tucking the bottom ends under the pumpkin. Add the flowers, cattails and leaves. Refer to the color photo for placement help. When you are happy with the placement, fuse in place. Add the word "Harvest" and fuse in place.

🍂 Lay the frame face down on the floor. Insert the appliquéd piece face down and then lay the batting on top of the appliquéd piece. Put the frame back in place. Hang and enjoy!

Harvest Framed Art
Made by Avis Shirer
Frame Size – 11¾" x 36"

Winter

❄

Old Fashioned Christmas

58" x 74"

There's something about the simplicity of a quilt made with red and green and muslin. It just takes me back to Christmas at Grandma's. What wonderful memories! Our machine quilter added so much to this quilt by quilting holly leaves and berries in the muslin rectangles—a perfect, final touch.

FABRIC REQUIREMENTS

1/3 yard each of 5 assorted reds
   for Flying Geese blocks

2 1/4 yards of muslin or tan solid

1/4 yard each of 4 assorted greens
   for inner block strips

2/3 yard of red tonal stripe
   for outer block strips

1/3 yard of green print for inner border

1 1/8 yards of mottled red solid for outer border

5/8 yard of red plaid for binding

Batting and backing measuring 64" x 80"

INSTRUCTIONS

Construct the Blocks

❄ Make 12 blocks. Finished size – 16" square.

For each block, Cut the following:

❄ Cut 2 – 5¼" squares, bisected twice to yield 8 triangles, from a red fabric – piece A

❄ Cut 8 – 2⅞" squares, bisected once to yield 16 triangles, from a red fabric – piece B

❄ Cut 2 – 5¼" squares, bisected twice to yield 8 triangles, from tan – piece C

❄ Cut 8 – 2⅞" squares, bisected once to yield 16 triangles, from tan – piece D

❄ Cut 1 – 4½" x 16½" rectangle from tan – piece E

❄ Cut 2 – 1½" x 16½" rectangles from green – piece F

❄ Cut 2 – 1½" x 16½" rectangles from red tonal stripe – piece G

❄ Sew two D triangles to a red A triangle. Repeat to make 8 like this.

❄ Now sew two red B triangles to a tan C triangle. Make 8 like this.

❄ Sew these Flying Geese units together as shown. Make 2 like this.

Make 2 like this.

Old Fashioned Christmas
Made by Tammy Johnson; Quilted by Sue Urich
58" x 74"

Sew these units together with the remaining pieces as shown to complete the block.

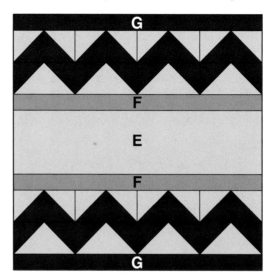

Assemble the Quilt

Sew the blocks together in four rows of three blocks each following the quilt diagram. For the inner border, cut 6 - 1½" wide strips across the width of the green fabric. Piece together and cut 2 – 1½" x 48½" strips and sew to the top and bottom of the quilt. Cut 2 – 1½" x 66½" and sew to the sides.

For the outer border, cut 7 – 4½" wide strips across the width of the mottled red fabric. Piece together and cut 2 – 4½" x 50½" strips and sew to the top and bottom of the quilt. Cut 2 – 4½" x 74½" strips and sew to the sides. Quilt as desired and bind. Refer to page 7 for more help with binding.

Vintage Christmas

33" x 42"

I love vintage ornaments! I am crazy about mercury glass and the soft, time worn colors. This quilt depicts some of those colors; soft blue, muted pink and rose with some rickrack and old buttons stitched on to complete the look.

FABRIC REQUIREMENTS

3/4 yard of light fabric for appliquéd blocks, outer corner blocks and outer border tongues

1/4 yard each of 3 assorted brown fabrics for baskets and outer border tongues

1/3 yard of soft red or deep rose plaid for pieced blocks

1/3 yard of dark pink print for pieced blocks

1/4 yard of light blue for inner border

1/4 yard of red for flower appliqués

1/4 yard of green for stem and leaf appliqués

1/8 yard of pink for flower centers

1/2 yard of floral for sashing strips

1 1/4 yard of yellow medium rickrack (if too bright, you can soften the color with tan dye)

1 1/2 yards of fusible web

42 white and off white buttons ranging in size from 5/8" to 7/8"

1/3 yard brown for binding

Brown embroidery floss

Batting and backing measuring 39" x 48"

INSTRUCTIONS

Appliqué Blocks

(Templates on page 77)

✤ Make 6 blocks. Finished size – 7" square.

✤ We used fusible appliqué throughout this project. For more information on fusible appliqué, refer to page 6. Cut six 7½" squares from the light fabric. Position the basket, centering it ⅜" up from the bottom raw edge of the square. Next, position the leaves and then add the stem on top. Tuck the raw edge of the stem under the basket. Next, add the flower and flower center. Refer to the color photo for placement help. When you are happy with the placement, fuse in place. Next, add the rickrack to the top of the baskets. Cut the rickrack approximately 6" to 6½" long. Turn the raw edges of the rickrack under so that the curves of the rickrack match. Stitch the rickrack in place with the brown embroidery floss. We used cross stitches but a simple running stitch could be used also.

Pieced Blocks

✤ Make 6 blocks. Finished size – 7" square.

To make all blocks:

✤ Cut 12 – 3⅞" squares, bisected once to yield 24 triangles, from soft red plaid – piece A.

✤ Cut 24 – 1½" x 3½" rectangles from soft red plaid – piece B

✤ Cut 12 – 3⅞" squares, bisected once to yield 24 triangles, from dark pink print – piece C

✤ Cut 6 – 1½" squares from dark pink print – piece D

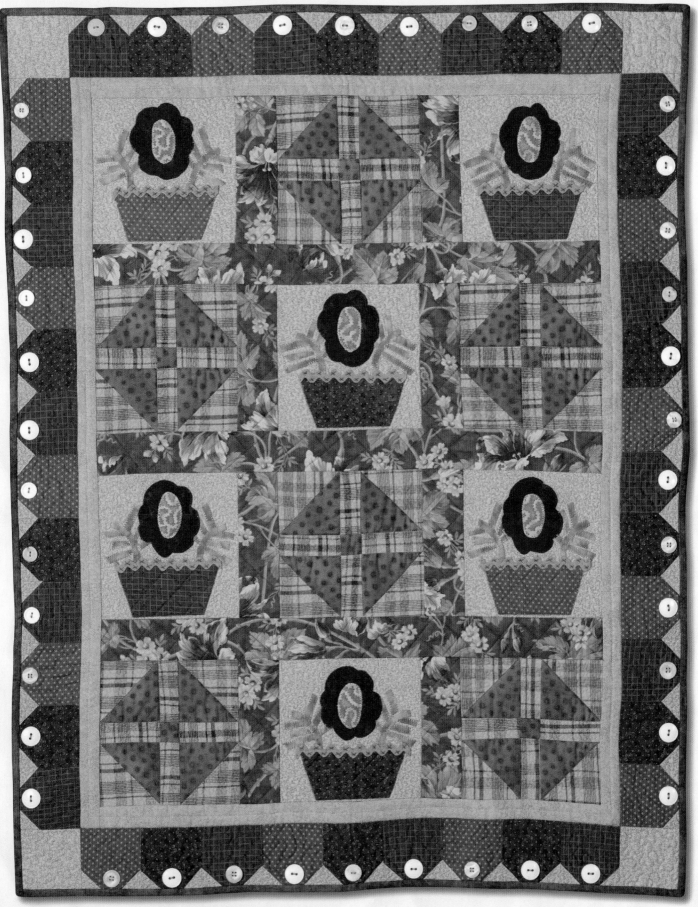

Vintage Christmas
Made by Avis Shirer
33" x 42"

Vintage Christmas continued

Sew these pieces together following the diagram.

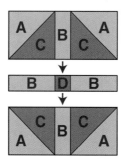

Assemble the Blocks

Cut 8 – 2 ½" x 7 ½" sashing strips from the floral fabric – piece A.

Cut 3 – 2 ½" x 25 ½" sashing strips from the floral fabric – piece B.

Sew these pieces and the blocks together following the diagram.

Borders

❊ For the inner border, cut 2 – 1 ½" x 25 ½" from the blue fabric. Sew to the top and bottom of the quilt. Cut 2 – 1 ½" x 36 ½" and sew to the sides.

For the outer border, cut the following:

❊ Cut 4 – 3 ½" squares from the light background fabric – piece A
❊ Cut 84 – 1 ½" squares from the light background fabric – piece B
❊ Cut 42 – 3 ½" squares from the assorted brown fabrics – piece C
❊ Lay a light B square on top of a brown C piece as shown. Stitch and flip following the instructions on page 6 for more information. Repeat with another light B square as shown. Repeat to make 42 of these units.

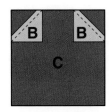 

❊ Stitch together two rows with nine blocks each. Sew to the top and bottom of the quilt. Stitch together two rows with 12 blocks each. Add a light A square to both ends and then stitch to the sides of the quilt. Quilt as desired and bind. For help with binding, refer to page 7 for more information.
❊ Stitch a button to each of the brown border tongues. These can be stitched on with your sewing machine. Refer to the owner's manual that came with your machine for complete instructions.

Joy

Frame size – 11 ¾" x 36"

I love decorating the house for Christmas. Tinsel trees, mercury glass, cherished ornaments that the boys made – they all make me happy but filling the house with family and friends makes me joyous!

FABRIC REQUIREMENTS

1/2 yard of cream background fabric

9" square of black wool or cotton for pot

2" x 18" piece of brown wool or cotton
   for tree trunk

9" square of green wool or cotton for branches

9" square of dark gray wool or cotton for letters
   and ornament tops

4" x 8" piece of pink wool or cotton
   for ornaments

10" x 15" piece of red wool or cotton
   for tongues and ornament stripes

1 yard of fusible web

11 3/4" x 36" piece of batting

Poster frame with an 11 3/4" x 36" opening

INSTRUCTIONS

Appliqué

(Templates on pages 78, 79)

✻ We used fusible appliqué throughout this project. Refer to page 6 for help with fusible appliqué. Cut an 11 ¾" x 36" rectangle from the cream background fabric. Lightly pencil in a line ¼" in from the sides and ¼" in from the top and bottom of the background piece as shown.

✻ Position seven red tongues at each end, using lines as a placement guide. Fuse in place.

✻ Position the remaining shapes before fusing in place so you can adjust the placement if necessary. Position the pot and pot rim, centering it ½" up from the bottom row of tongues. For the tree trunk, draw a ¾" x 15 ½" rectangle on the paper side of the fusible web. Cut outside the drawn line and fuse to the brown wool or cotton. Cut out on the line and position it down the center of the background piece and tucking the bottom end under the pot rim. Position the three branches and the two ornaments, tucking the top of the ornament hangers under the branches. Finally, position the word "JOY." When you are happy with the placement, fuse in place.

✻ Lay the frame face down on the floor. Insert the appliquéd piece face down and then lay the batting on top of the appliquéd piece. Put the frame back in place. Hang and enjoy!

Joy Framed Art
Frame size – 11 ¾" x 36"
Made by Tammy Johnson

Edna's Vines

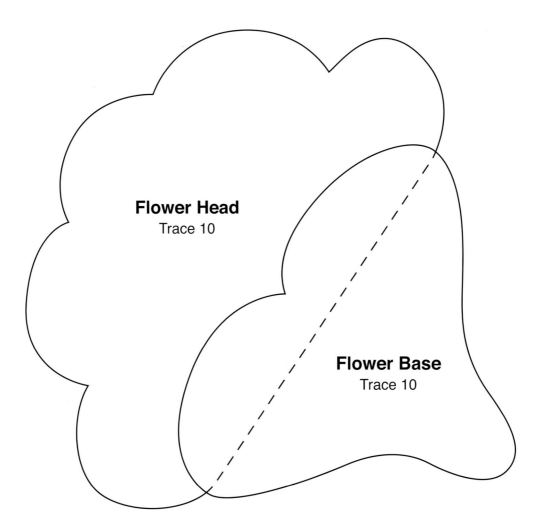

Flower Head
Trace 10

Flower Base
Trace 10

All templates have
been reversed for
fusible applique.

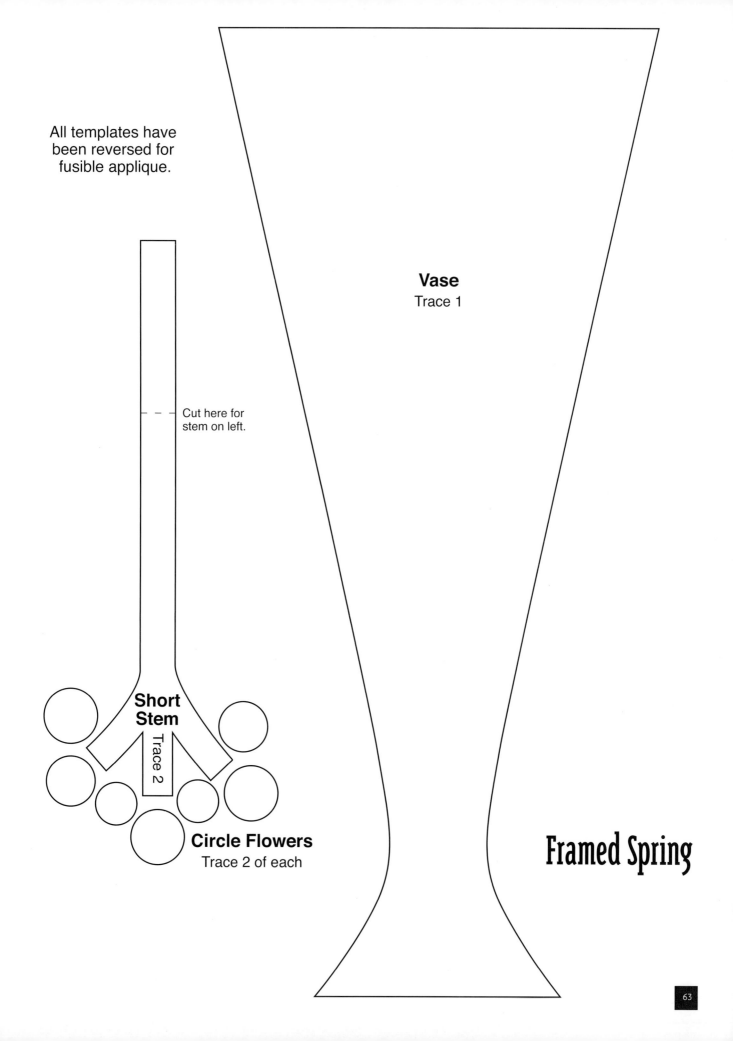

All templates have been reversed for fusible applique.

Vase
Trace 1

Cut here for stem on left.

Short Stem
Trace 2

Circle Flowers
Trace 2 of each

Framed Spring

63

Framed Spring

All templates have
been reversed for
fusible applique.

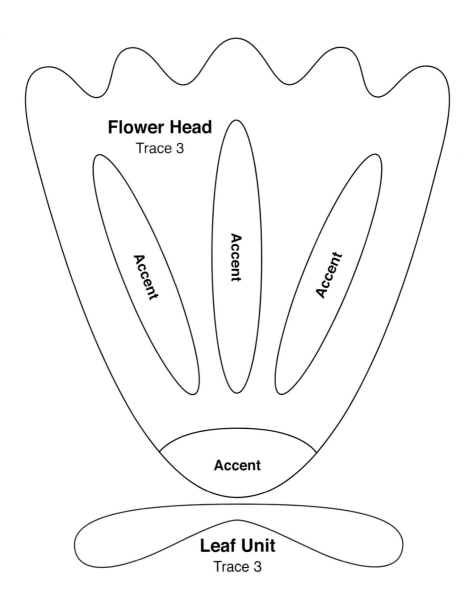

Flower Head
Trace 3

Accent

Accent

Accent

Accent

Leaf Unit
Trace 3

The stem measurements are:
Left stem - 3/8" x 5 1/2"
Center stem - 3/8" x 10"
Right stem - 3/8" x 7 1/2"

Dahlia

To make complete basket
template, attach basket
from following pattern page.

Dotted lines
for position only.

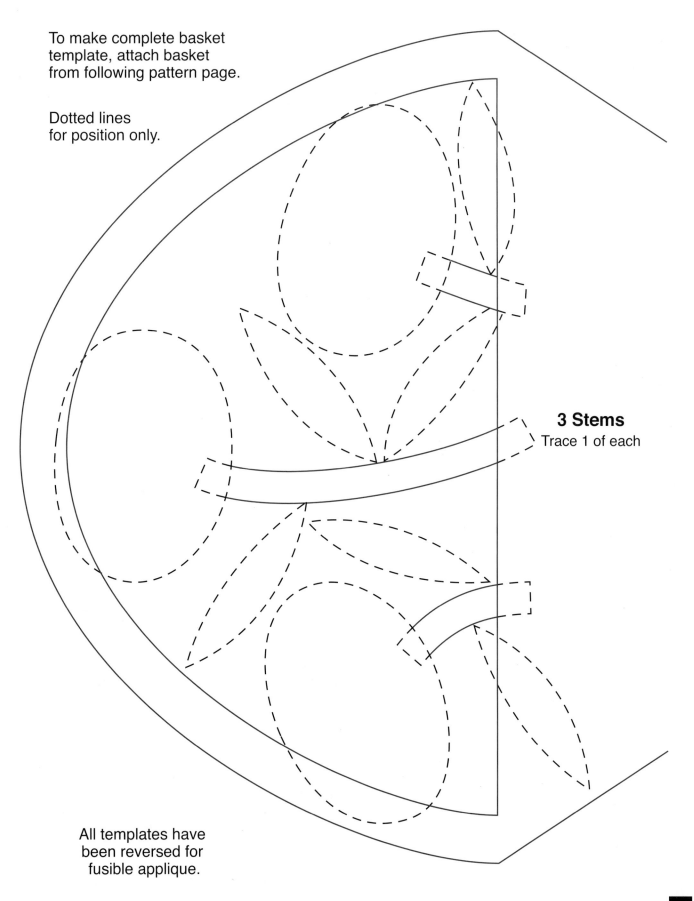

3 Stems
Trace 1 of each

All templates have
been reversed for
fusible applique.

Dahlia

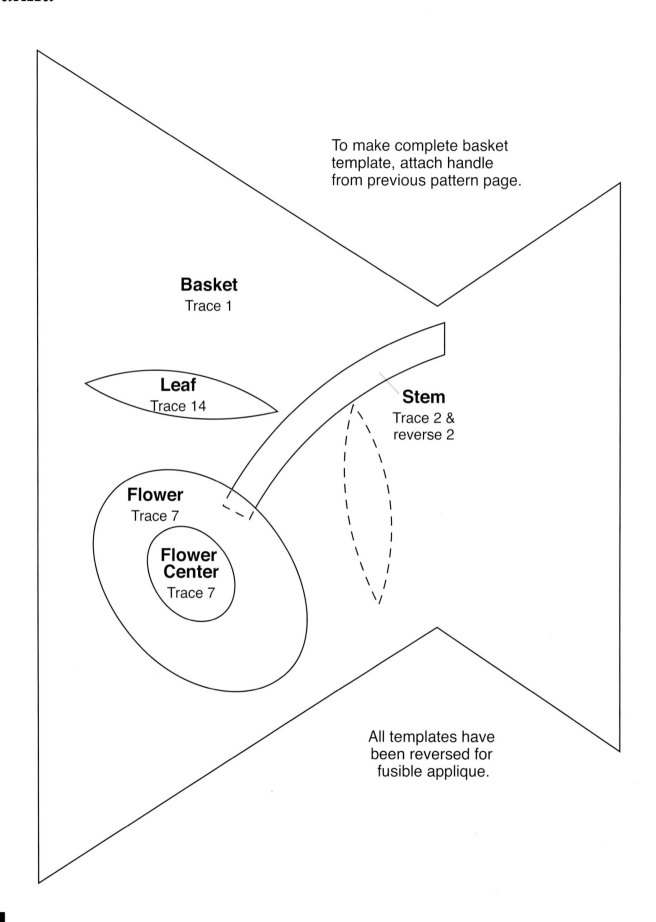

To make complete basket template, attach handle from previous pattern page.

Basket
Trace 1

Leaf
Trace 14

Stem
Trace 2 & reverse 2

Flower
Trace 7

Flower Center
Trace 7

All templates have been reversed for fusible applique.

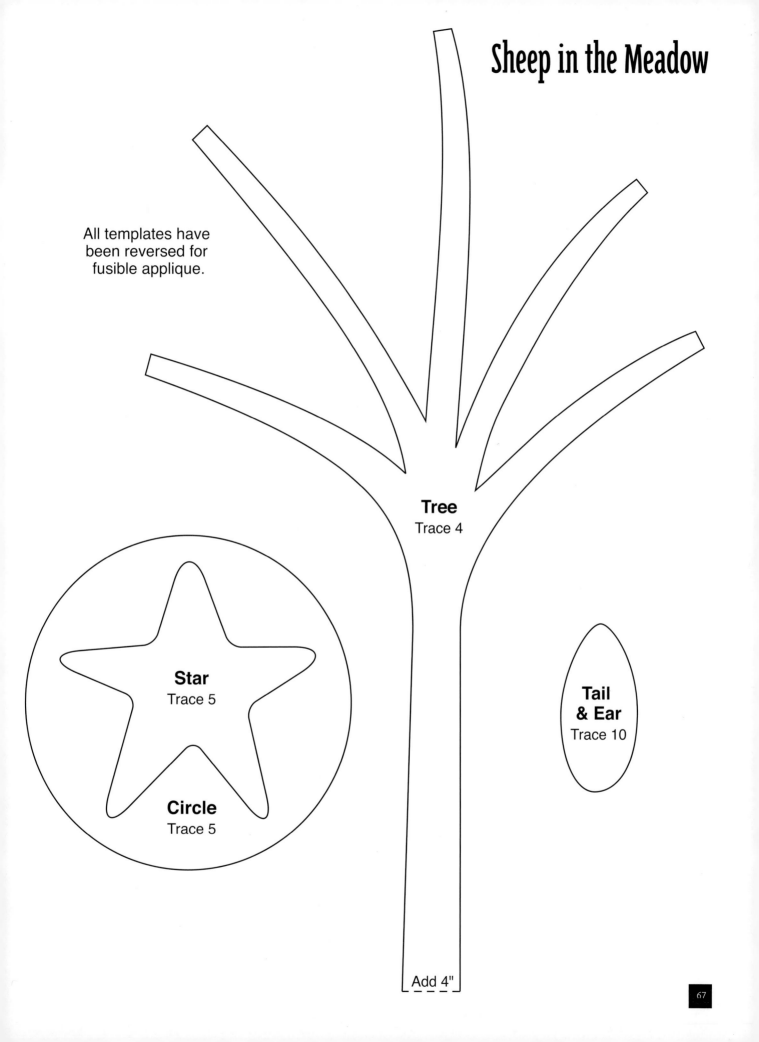

Sheep in the Meadow

All templates have been reversed for fusible applique.

Tree
Trace 4

Star
Trace 5

Circle
Trace 5

Tail & Ear
Trace 10

Add 4"

Liberty Framed Art

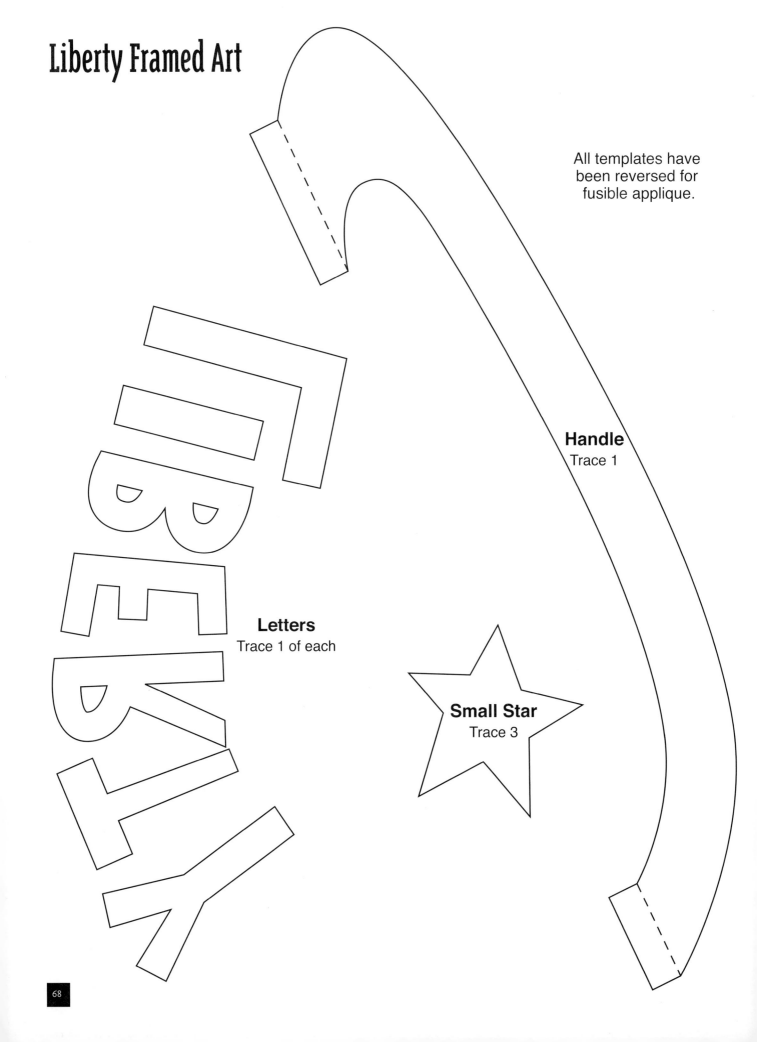

All templates have
been reversed for
fusible applique.

Handle
Trace 1

Letters
Trace 1 of each

Small Star
Trace 3

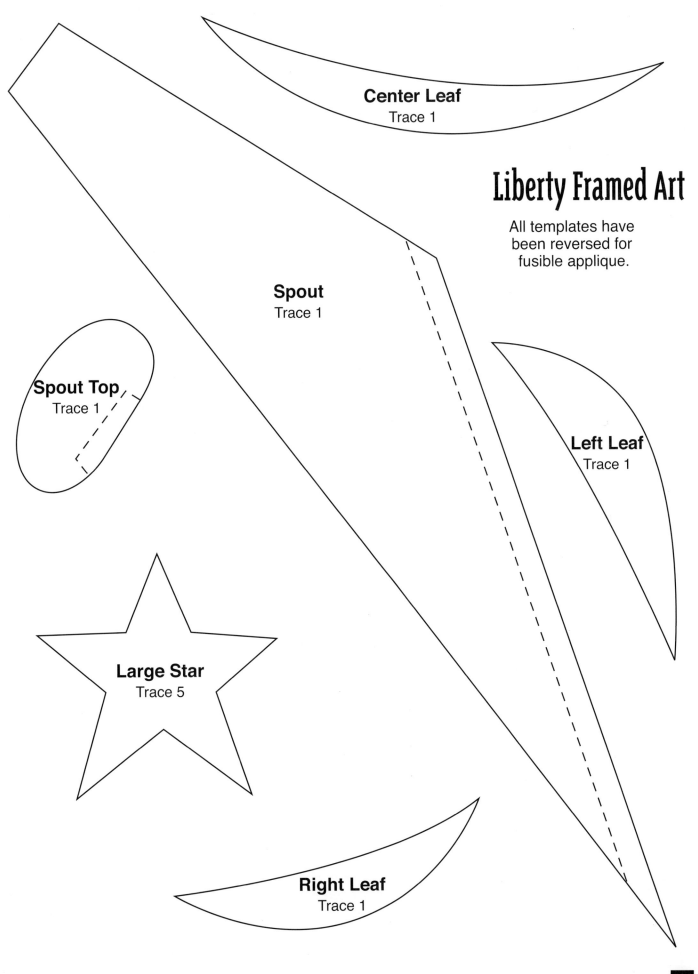

Center Leaf
Trace 1

Liberty Framed Art

All templates have been reversed for fusible applique.

Spout
Trace 1

Spout Top
Trace 1

Left Leaf
Trace 1

Large Star
Trace 5

Right Leaf
Trace 1

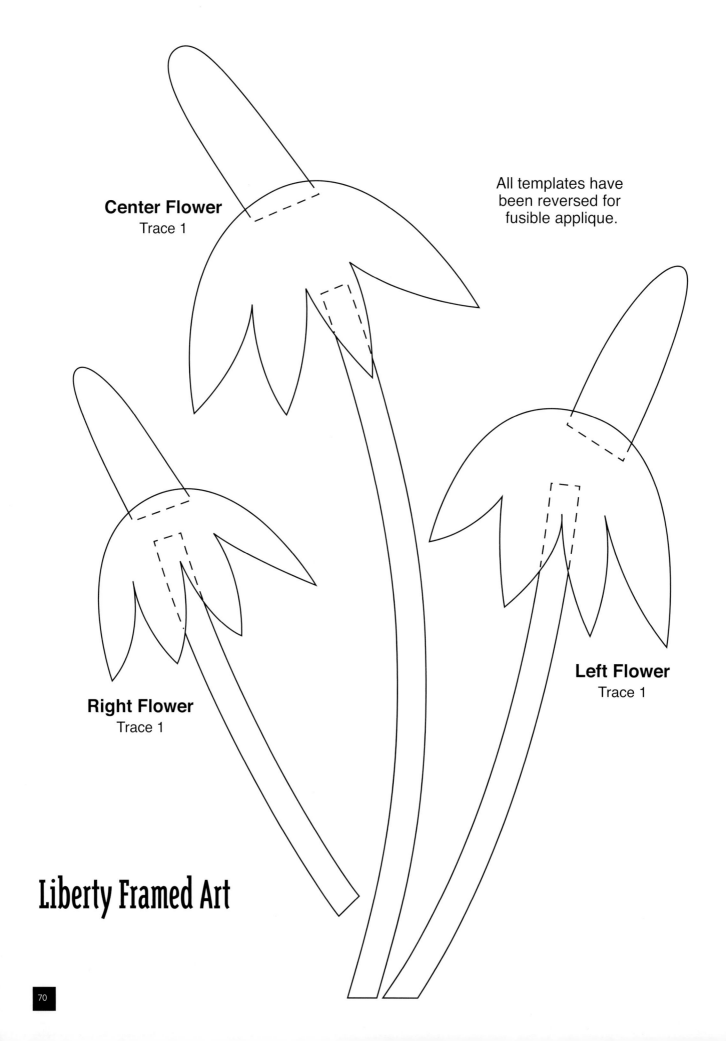

Center Flower
Trace 1

All templates have
been reversed for
fusible applique.

Right Flower
Trace 1

Left Flower
Trace 1

Liberty Framed Art

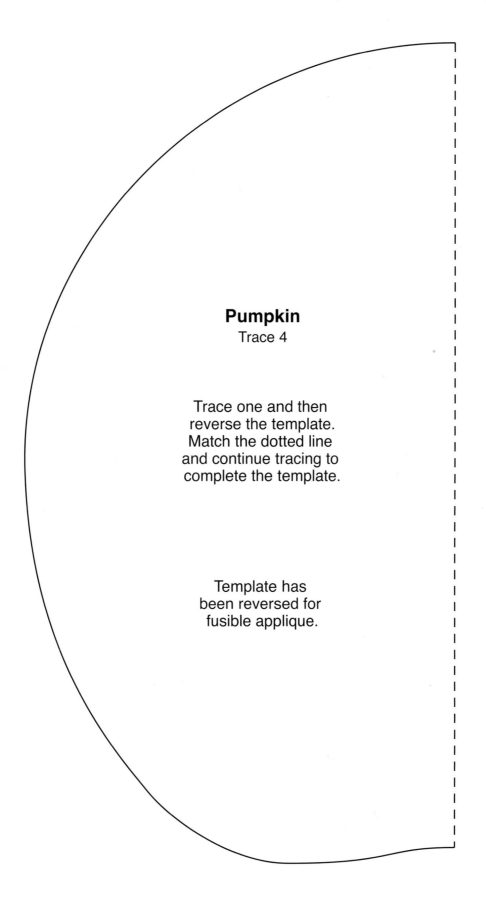

Pumpkin
Trace 4

Trace one and then
reverse the template.
Match the dotted line
and continue tracing to
complete the template.

Template has
been reversed for
fusible applique.

Pumpkins and Acorns Galore

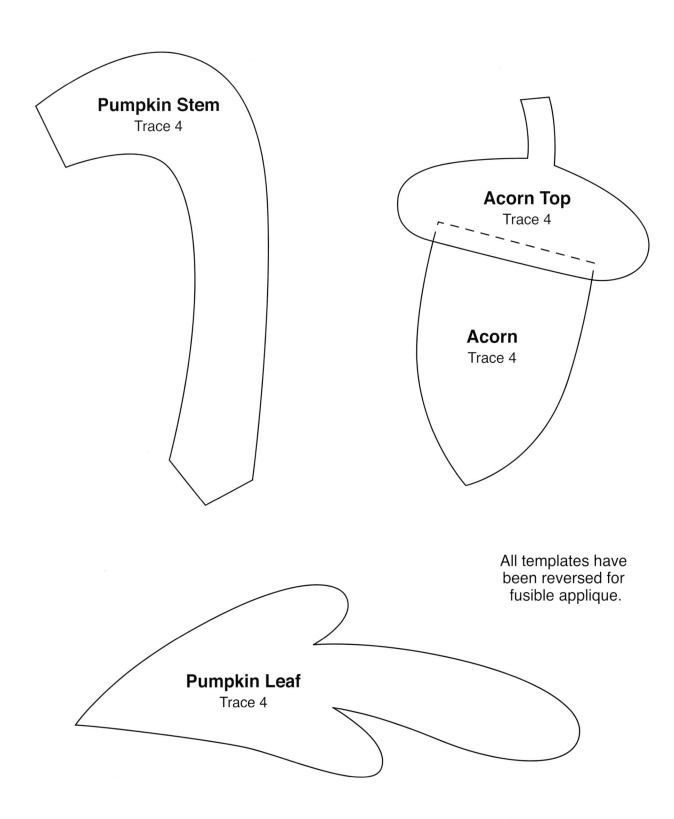

Pumpkin Stem
Trace 4

Acorn Top
Trace 4

Acorn
Trace 4

All templates have been reversed for fusible applique.

Pumpkin Leaf
Trace 4

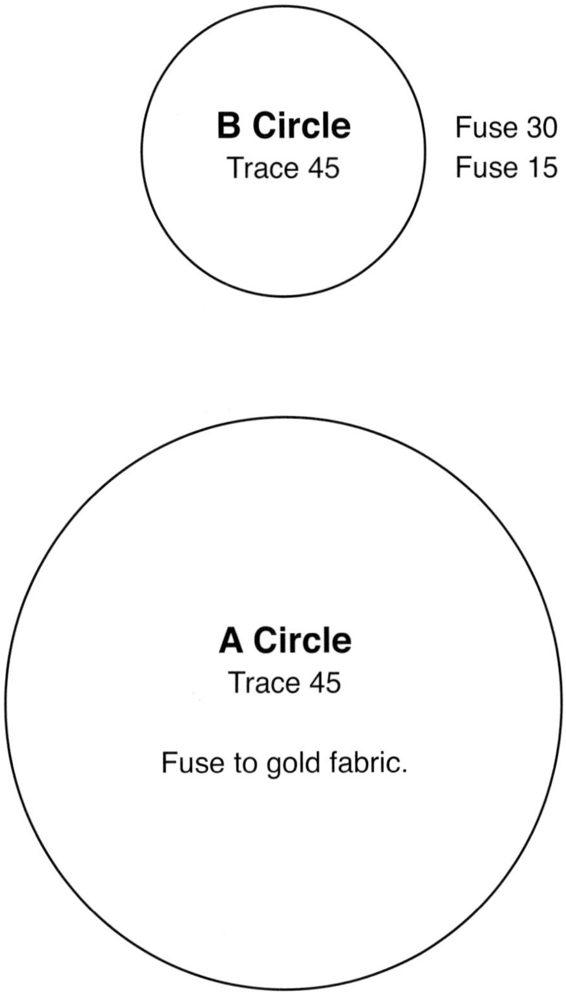

B Circle

Trace 45

Fuse 30 to blue fabric
Fuse 15 to rust fabric

A Circle

Trace 45

Fuse to gold fabric.

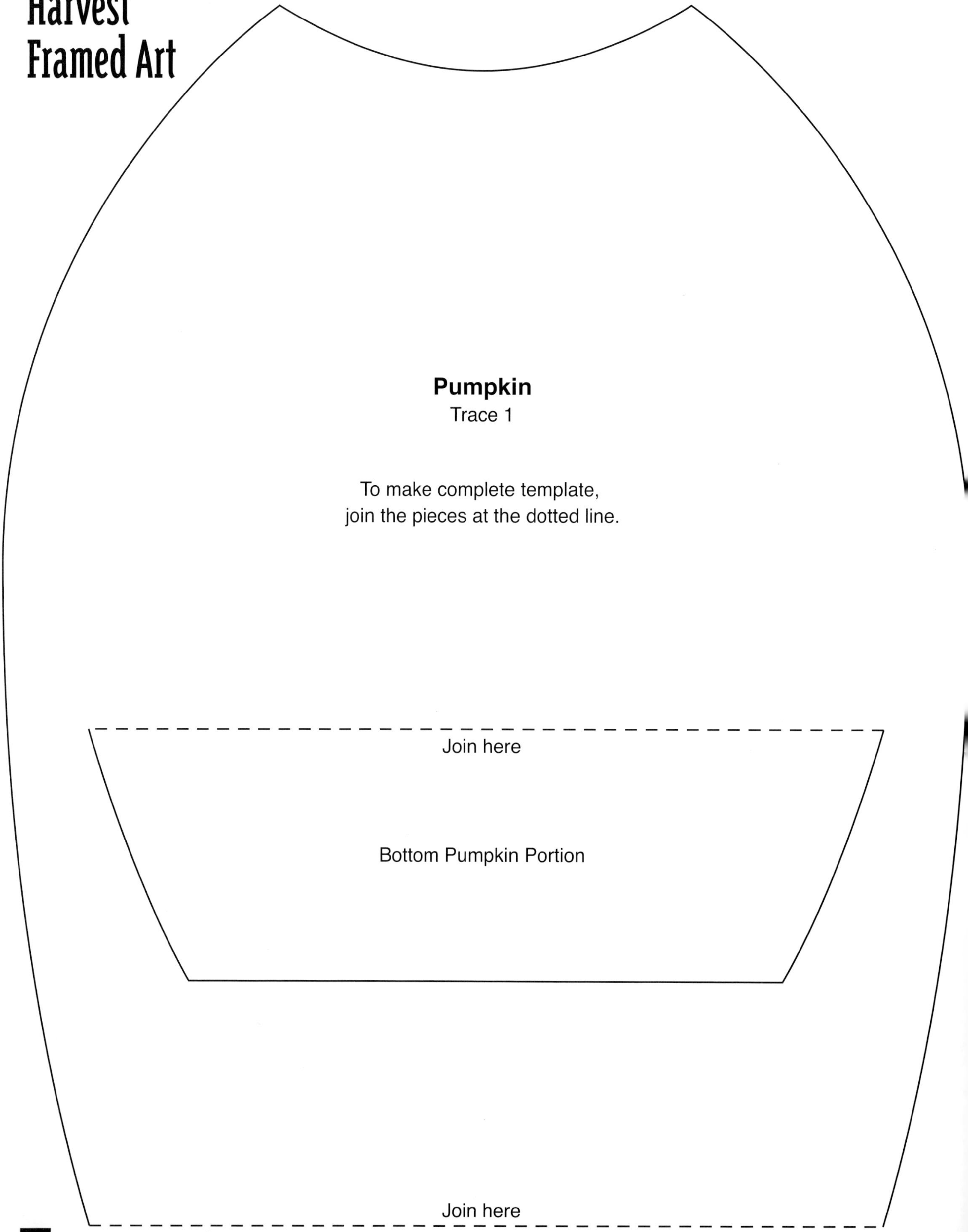

Pumpkin
Trace 1

To make complete template,
join the pieces at the dotted line.

Join here

Bottom Pumpkin Portion

Join here

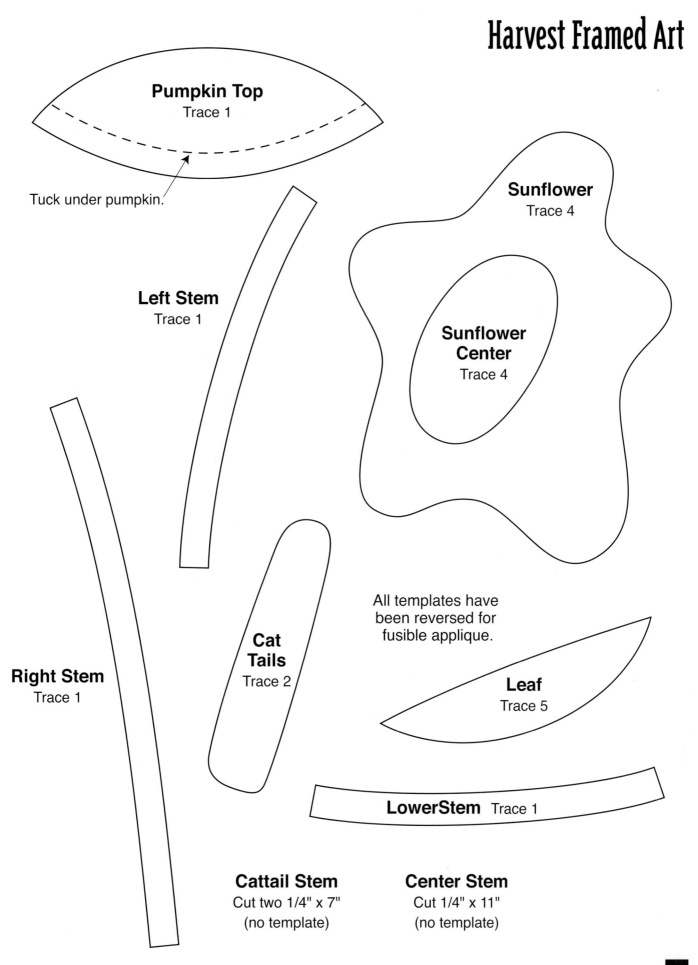

Harvest Framed Art

Pumpkin Top
Trace 1

Tuck under pumpkin.

Left Stem
Trace 1

Sunflower
Trace 4

Sunflower Center
Trace 4

Right Stem
Trace 1

Cat Tails
Trace 2

All templates have been reversed for fusible applique.

Leaf
Trace 5

LowerStem Trace 1

Cattail Stem
Cut two 1/4" x 7"
(no template)

Center Stem
Cut 1/4" x 11"
(no template)

Harvest Framed Art

Letters have been reversed for fusible applique.

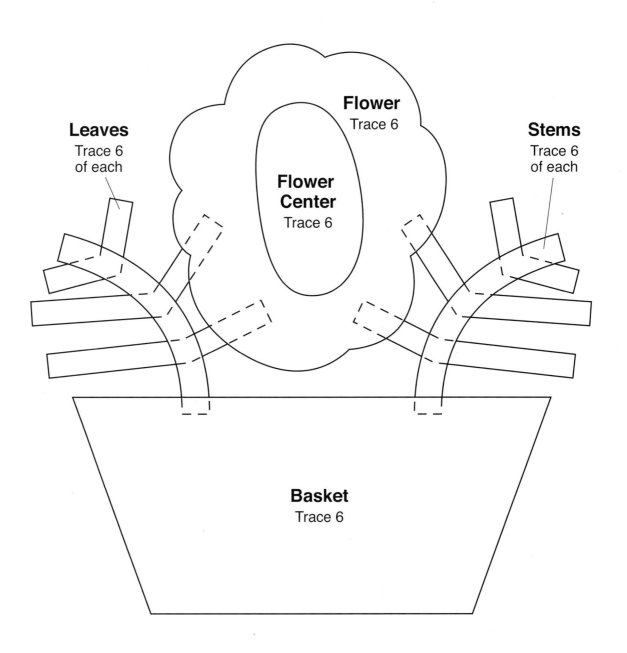

Flower
Trace 6

Leaves
Trace 6
of each

**Flower
Center**
Trace 6

Stems
Trace 6
of each

Basket
Trace 6

All templates have
been reversed for
fusible applique.

Joy Framed Art

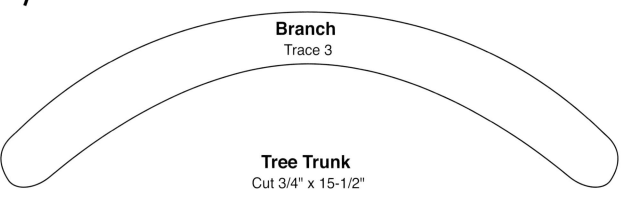

Branch
Trace 3

Tree Trunk
Cut 3/4" x 15-1/2"

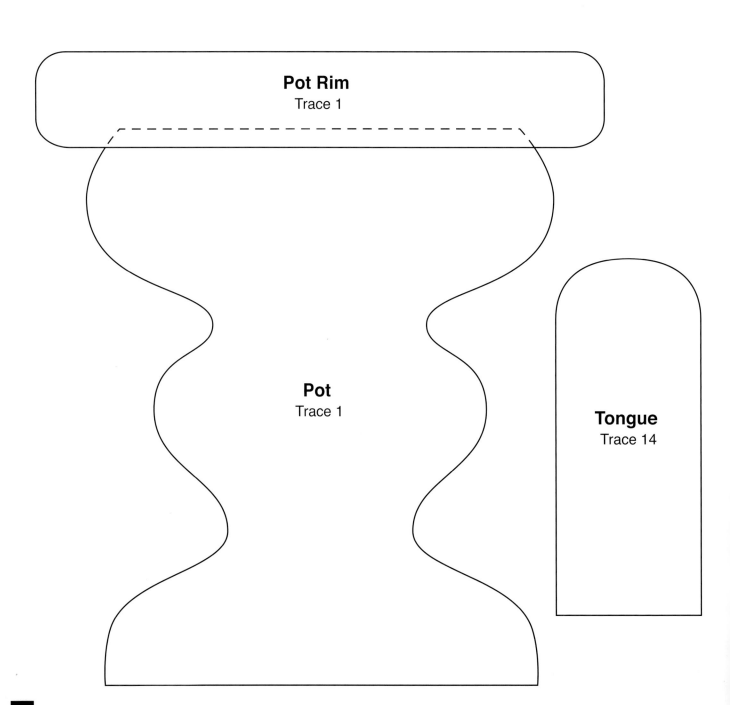

Pot Rim
Trace 1

Pot
Trace 1

Tongue
Trace 14

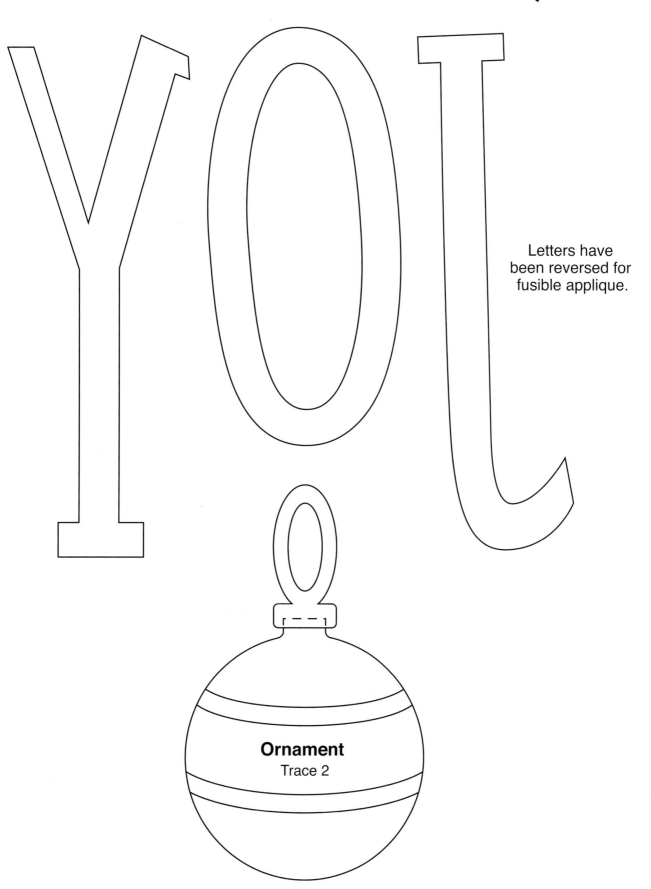

Letters have
been reversed for
fusible applique.

Ornament
Trace 2

Other Star Books

New in 2009

Flora Botanica: Quilts from the Spencer Museum of Art
by Barbara Brackman – 2009

Making Memories: Simple Quilts from Cherished Clothing
by Deb Rowden – 2009

Pots de Fleurs: A Garden of Applique Techniques by Kathy Delaney – 2009

Wedding Ring, Pickle Dish and More: Paper Piecing Curves
by Carolyn McCormick – 2009

The Graceful Garden: A Jacobean Fantasy Quilt
by Denise Sheehan – 2009

My Stars: Patterns from The Kansas City Star, Volume I – 2009

Opening Day: 14 Quilts Celebrating the Life and Times of Negro Leagues Baseball by Sonie Ruffin – 2009

St. Louis Stars: Nine Unique Quilts that Spark by Toby Lischko – 2009

Whimsyland: Be Cre8ive with Lizzie B by Liz & Beth Hawkins – 2009

From Our Collection

Quilts in Red and Green and the Women Who Made Them
by Nancy Hornback and Terry Clothier Thompson – 2006

Hard Times, Splendid Quilts: A 1930s Celebration, Paper Piecing from The Kansas City Star by Carolyn Cullinan McCormick – 2006

Art Nouveau Quilts for the 21st Century by Bea Oglesby – 2006

Designer Quilts: Great Projects from Moda's Best Fabric Artists – 2006

Birds of a Feather by Barb Adams and Alma Allen – 2006

Feedsacks! Beautiful Quilts from Humble Beginnings
by Edie McGinnis – 2006

Kansas Spirit: Historical Quilt Blocks and the Saga of the Sunflower State
by Jeanne Poore – 2006

Bold Improvisation: Searching for African-American Quilts – The Heffley Collection by Scott Heffley – 2007

The Soulful Art of African-American Quilts: Nineteen Bold, Improvisational Projects by Sonie Ruffin – 2007

Alphabet Quilts: Letters for All Ages by Bea Oglesby – 2007

Beyond the Basics: A Potpourri of Quiltmaking Techniques
by Kathy Delaney – 2007

Golden's Journal: 20 Sampler Blocks Honoring Prairie Farm Life
by Christina DeArmond, Eula Lang and Kaye Spitzli – 2007

Borderland in Butternut and Blue: A Sampler Quilt to Recall the Civil War Along the Kansas/Missouri Border by Barbara Brackman – 2007

Come to the Fair: Quilts that Celebrate State Fair Traditions
by Edie McGinnis – 2007

Cotton and Wool: Miss Jump's Farewell by Linda Brannock – 2007

You're Invited! Quilts and Homes to Inspire
by Barb Adams and Alma Allen, Blackbird Designs – 2007

Portable Patchwork: Who Says You Can't Take it With You?
by Donna Thomas – 2008

Quilts for Rosie: Paper Piecing Patterns from the '40s
by Carolyn Cullinan McCormick – 2008

Fruit Salad: Appliqué Designs for Delicious Quilts by Bea Oglesby – 2008

Red, Green and Beyond by Nancy Hornback
and Terry Clothier Thompson – 2008

A Dusty Garden Grows by Terry Clothier Thompson – 2008

We Gather Together: A Harvest of Quilts by Jan Patek – 2008

With These Hands: 19th Century-Inspired Primitive Projects for Your Home
by Maggie Bonanomi – 2008

As the Cold Wind Blows by Barb Adams and Alma Allen – 2008

Caring for Your Quilts: Textile Conservation, Repair and Storage
by Hallye Bone – 2008

The Circuit Rider's Quilt: An Album Quilt Honoring a Beloved Minister
by Jenifer Dick – 2008

Embroidered Quilts: From Hands and Hearts by Christina DeArmond,
Eula Lang and Kaye Spitzli – 2008

Reminiscing: A Whimsicals Collections by Terri Degenkolb – 2008

Scraps and Shirttails: Reuse, Re-purpose and Recycle! The Art of Green Quilting by Bonnie Hunter – 2008

Queen Bees Mysteries

Murders on Elderberry Road by Sally Goldenbaum – 2003

A Murder of Taste by Sally Goldenbaum – 2004

Murder on a Starry Night by Sally Goldenbaum – 2005

Dog-Gone Murder by Marnette Falley – 2008

Project Books

Fan Quilt Memories by Jeanne Poore – 2000

Santa's Parade of Nursery Rhymes by Jeanne Poore – 2001

As the Crow Flies by Edie McGinnis – 2007

Sweet Inspirations by Pam Manning – 2007

Quilts Through the Camera's Eye by Terry Clothier Thompson – 2007

Louisa May Alcott: Quilts of Her Life, Her Work, Her Heart
by Terry Clothier Thompson – 2008

The Lincoln Museum Quilt: A Reproduction for Abe's Frontier Cabin
by Barbara Brackman and Deb Rowden – 2008

Dinosaurs – Stomp, Chomp and Roar by Pam Manning – 2008

Carrie Hall's Sampler: Favorite Blocks from a Classic Pattern Collection
by Barbara Brackman – 2008

Just Desserts: Quick Quilts Using Pre-cut Fabrics
by Edie McGinnis – 2009

Christmas at Home: Quilts for Your Holiday Traditions by Christina
DeArmond, Eula Lang and Kaye Spitzli – 2009

Geese in the Rose Garden by Dawn Heese – 2009

DVD Project

The Kansas City Stars: A Quilting Legacy – 2008